THE WORLD OF TURNER

PAVILION
MICHAEL JOSEPH

First published in Great Britain in 1989 by
Pavilion Books Limited
196 Shaftesbury Avenue, London WC2H 8JL
in association with Michael Joseph Limited
27 Wrights Lane, Kensington, London W8 5TZ

Designed by Bridgewater Design Limited

ISBN: 1-85145-453-5

Printed and bound in Singapore by Imago Publishing Limited

10 9 8 7 6 5 4 3 2 1

FOREWORD

*T*he career of J.M.W. Turner (1775-1851) spanned a period of rapid change and his work represents an organic link between the academic and classical traditions of the eighteenth century and modern art. Yet only in our own day have his range and stature been fully appreciated.

The precocious young painter who began as a topographical watercolourist was equally receptive to such contrasting influences as Claude, Poussin, the Dutch marine school and the Italian masters. Through study, observation and travel he absorbed them into a unique personal synthesis which he never ceased to develop. In Turner's art all subject-matter, whether classical, historical or contemporary, is related to the landscape, and subordinated to the dramatic and often violent effects of nature. It was above all the problem of light which occupied him, whether in the tranquility of his dreamlike Venetian scenes, the awesome fury of his storms, or the increasing abstraction of later work such as *Norham Castle, Sunrise*. Technically he can now be seen to anticipate many aspects of modern art but in his lyricism, his sense of the tragic, his fascination with the dramatic and sublime, he was by temperament a Romantic.

Turner's final gesture was to bequeath his entire studio collection to the nation, with the condition that it should all be housed together. When the Tate Gallery, by Turner's beloved Thames, opened the Clore Gallery for this purpose in 1987, the cantankerous old hero of English painting at last received his due.

J . M . W . TURNER (1775-1851)
Sunrise with Sea Monsters (c. 1845)
THE TATE GALLERY, LONDON

PUBLISHED BY PAVILION BOOKS LIMITED

J . M . W . TURNER (1775-1851)
The Sun of Venice going to Sea (exh. 1843)
THE TATE GALLERY, LONDON

PUBLISHED BY PAVILION BOOKS LIMITED

J . M . W . TURNER (1775-1851)
Shipping off East Cowes Headland (1827)
THE TATE GALLERY, LONDON

PUBLISHED BY PAVILION BOOKS LIMITED

J . M . W . T U R N E R (1775-1851)
Childe Harold's Pilgrimage: Italy (exh. 1832)
THE TATE GALLERY, LONDON

PUBLISHED BY PAVILION BOOKS LIMITED

J . M . W . T U R N E R (1775-1851)
Mercury sent to admonish Aeneas (exh. 1850)
THE TATE GALLERY, LONDON

PUBLISHED BY PAVILION BOOKS LIMITED

J . M . W . T U R N E R (1775-1851)
Heidelberg (c. 1840-5)
THE TATE GALLERY, LONDON

PUBLISHED BY PAVILION BOOKS LIMITED

J . M . W . T U R N E R (1775-1851)
Fishermen at Sea (exh. 1796)
THE TATE GALLERY, LONDON

PUBLISHED BY PAVILION BOOKS LIMITED

J . M . W . TURNER (1775-1851)
Buttermere Lake, with part of Cromackwater, Cumberland, a Shower
(exh. 1798)
THE TATE GALLERY, LONDON

PUBLISHED BY PAVILION BOOKS LIMITED

J . M . W . T U R N E R (1775-1851)
The Dogana, San Giorgio, Citella, from Steps of the Europa (exh. 1842)
THE TATE GALLERY, LONDON

PUBLISHED BY PAVILION BOOKS LIMITED

J . M . W . TURNER (1775-1851)
A Fire at Sea (?c. 1835)
THE TATE GALLERY, LONDON

PUBLISHED BY PAVILION BOOKS LIMITED

J . M . W . T U R N E R (1775-1851)
View of Orvieto, painted in Rome (1828)
THE TATE GALLERY, LONDON

P U B L I S H E D B Y P A V I L I O N B O O K S L I M I T E D

J . M . W . T U R N E R (1775-1851)
The Bay of Baiae, with Apollo and the Sibyl (exh. 1823)
THE TATE GALLERY, LONDON

PUBLISHED BY PAVILION BOOKS LIMITED

J . M . W . T U R N E R (1775-1851)
Whalers (exh. 1845)
THE TATE GALLERY, LONDON

PUBLISHED BY PAVILION BOOKS LIMITED

PUBLISHED BY PAVILION BOOKS LIMITED

J . M . W . TURNER (1775-1851)
Coast Scene near Naples (?1828)
THE TATE GALLERY, LONDON

PUBLISHED BY PAVILION BOOKS LIMITED

J . M . W . T U R N E R (1775-1851)
Ploughing up Turnips, near Slough ('Windsor') (exh. 1809)
THE TATE GALLERY, LONDON

PUBLISHED BY PAVILION BOOKS LIMITED

J . M . W . TURNER (1775-1851)
George IV at the Provost's Banquet in the Parliament House, Edinburgh
(c. 1822)
THE TATE GALLERY, LONDON

PUBLISHED BY PAVILION BOOKS LIMITED

PUBLISHED BY PAVILION BOOKS LIMITED

J . M . W . T U R N E R (1775-1851)
Ancient Rome; Agrippina landing with the Ashes of Germanicus (exh. 1839)
THE TATE GALLERY, LONDON

PUBLISHED BY PAVILION BOOKS LIMITED

J . M . W . TURNER (1775-1851)
Sunrise, with a boat between Headlands (c. 1840-5)
THE TATE GALLERY, LONDON

PUBLISHED BY PAVILION BOOKS LIMITED

J . M . W . T U R N E R (1775-1851)
St. Benedetto, looking towards Fusina (exh. 1843)
THE TATE GALLERY, LONDON

PUBLISHED BY PAVILION BOOKS LIMITED

J . M . W . T U R N E R (1775-1851)
Procession of Boats with Distant Smoke, Venice (c. 1845)
THE TATE GALLERY, LONDON

PUBLISHED BY PAVILION BOOKS LIMITED

J . M . W . T U R N E R (1775–1851)
Tivoli: Tobias and the Angel (c. 1835)
THE TATE GALLERY, LONDON

PUBLISHED BY PAVILION BOOKS LIMITED

J . M . W . T U R N E R (1775-1851)
Rome, from the Vatican. Raffaelle, accompanied by La Fornarina, preparing his Pictures for the Decoration of the Loggia (exh. 1820)
THE TATE GALLERY, LONDON

P U B L I S H E D   B Y   P A V I L I O N   B O O K S   L I M I T E D

J . M . W . TURNER (1775-1851)
Bridge of Sighs, Ducal Palace and Custom-House, Venice: Canaletti Painting (exh. 1833)
THE TATE GALLERY, LONDON

PUBLISHED BY PAVILION BOOKS LIMITED

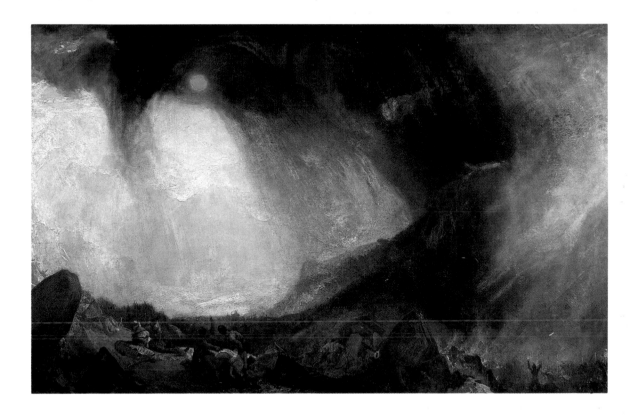

J . M . W . TURNER (1775-1851)
Snowstorm: Hannibal and his Army crossing the Alps (exh. 1812)
THE TATE GALLERY, LONDON

PUBLISHED BY PAVILION BOOKS LIMITED

J . M . W . TURNER (1775-1851)
Norham Castle, Sunrise (c. 1845)
THE TATE GALLERY, LONDON

PUBLISHED BY PAVILION BOOKS LIMITED